Come Sway
With Me

Tanya Raval

Dedication

To:

An artist,

A righteous, perseverant, and sensitive soul,

The best father,

R.T. Raval

Acknowledgment

Compiling what was written in my journals into this book would not have been possible without the help of my loving family – they put up with my eccentricities! Many thanks are due to my parents, whose unconditional love and individualistic upbringing brought out the best in my siblings and me. Thanks to my dear sisters whose love and support have seen me through the bitter blue days. My dear friend Anjali's support and friendly chatter during the early days of healing made me feel safe and vulnerable. I am also grateful to Anita for her support. It has made a fruitful ending possible for this, my labor of love.

Tanya Raval

Contents

Introduction

During childhood and middle school, my desire to express euphoria and sadness as hyperbole was meagerly satisfied by the language class where essay writing was compulsory. The intensity of my feelings was not always allowed to be expressed because of cultural restraints. I was born a girl who must always be quite subdued and polite. These expectations were not too demanding or different from the experiences of my friends and peers. However, I could not always curtail the desire to be vociferous about the upsurge of emotions that I felt. What nonsense to have a wandering mind easily wanting to hide in the realms of a fantasy world! Retrospective understanding now helps me see how my emotions are tied as they were to a galloping mind with fast-firing neurons. I could not fathom how they were being tamed and regulated without counseling. Mind management was a taboo in Indian society; it was aided by a lack of awareness of the need for intervention by psychiatry. One did not receive counseling. Unless one was just simply MAD, this left confused parents alone to manage a temperamental child. How I survived those years is not just a miracle. It is also a justification for the social glue that extended family life provides. If the parents could not curtail my childish tantrums, the uncle was always around to distract my mind from the gnawing ache of not being understood or allowing me to be in the present. Nevertheless, even with the help of extended family, bottling up the effervescence of emotions became the inevitable consequence.

In my later adult years, when I was cajoled and coaxed by extended family members, the need for psychiatry became obvious. At first, the fight from within was without. I resisted the court orders for medication, arguing against them by using my advanced education and training in science, specifically, my knowledge of biochemical and signal transduction pathways, being a network of connections. A drug-like compound pushing the pathway in one direction would cause an imbalance in the other pathway. My argument was congruent with the lack of diagnostic methods to show an imbalance in the neurotransmitters in the first place, to require an exogenous supply or inhibit its reuptake (Serotonin reuptake inhibitors). It was difficult to convince me without evidence that I needed what I had less of or that I had more of something that had to be diminished. Counseling was the early choice of acceptance that I needed help with.

The first counseling sessions focused on discussing the past; they bored me to death. Later, I was taught the cognitive theory of behavior transformation (CTBT). The goal was to manage the mind to alter deleterious and negative thought patterns such that it results in a different action and response, and thereby brings about a change in behavior. For me, though, this was easier said than done! Until one fateful conversation.

The counselor asked me, "Do you journal your thoughts and actions for the day?"

The recalcitrant question flitted through my mind: "As it is, I have trouble dealing with the feelings and emotions associated with an interaction or situation. Why would I want to reiterate this by writing it down and etching in my memory something that I dislike?"!

Aloud, I answered simply, monosyllabically: "No."

Undaunted, the counsellor persevered. "Maybe if you write down how intensely you feel something, it may dampen and reduce the edge of the incident before you have to talk about it or relate to it."

Something inside of me responded. "Hmmm, I could give it a try."

Instead of writing incidents in prose, though, I decided to communicate my feelings strictly to myself in my journal as poems. That's what you'll find in this book: a collection of those thoughts.

In the process of my healing, I learned several techniques. Expungement of sorrow and anger, deep breathing, imagery, and cathartic writing as such follows.

Much later, my counselor's suggestion, to convert a negative thought into a positive feeling was accepted when I began to write something upbeat as well.

That is what you will find within the pages of this book. I present to you my efforts of thought transformations in an arrangement that shows the darkness of disparity and the glimmers of hope when the light breaks through. So come, sway with me through a journey of - down in the dumps of despair to the buoyancy of a solid hope.

Tell him.

Wandering in thought, I glaze over my reality.
A small bell ringing a dream of felicity,

A sound soft at first, a whisper,
Almost as if after he kissed her,

Staying in thought all through the night,
Ringing a toll bell of sirens, in silent fright

Louder and louder, coarser, and firmer, abusive and
commanding
My darkened plight succumbing,

Growing to a cacophony of noises
They say it is time for my medicines as my body poises,

A harsh flip on my bed as my butt pinches,
With unasked doses of stuff, not caring for my flinches,

He did this to me, as I was not so
Beckon him and tell him I know.

Coping

Depression and Paranoia are two opposite sides of a coin.
In depression, the world and you are separated,
Everyone falls apart, and you get isolated,
No one cares as they bare,
The processes of your thoughts and how they snare.

In paranoia, everything is centripetal.
And too many involved in your space and all in CAPITALS
They follow you and chase you.
Not knowing how it makes you PHEW!

So, keep calm and befriend many,

Humor yourself and accept your flaws,
Remember not to draw out your claws,

Seek help and be of service to others,
We are together in creation to be kindred.

Tanya Raval

Suction

Is this life? when sadness is greater than happiness?
Is this life? when inertia is more than change from bitterness?
Is this life when all potential tends to nothingness?

The kinetic energy is held up in a ball of fit-full emotions.
No one dared to talk to me in these conditions.

The feelings saturated my endocrines.
A hypoplasia, which everything shuns,
No fancies!

A funnel into
Darkness.

Am I going towards my source of grief attraction, OR
Sinking into the oblivion of black hole suction?

A Wonderful Day

Arise this morning with a smile,
The slumber dreams gone by awaken me agile.

This is going to be a wonderful day.
The sun has lit this morning of May.

The smell of washed sky and earth,
Cleansed of dusty mud from new birth.

The glory of color-bedecked flowers grove
The cool wind from the oceans comes to the shore.

The hummingbird fluttering its wings,
Telling me the story of bees without kings
The queen will carry the conquest of Honey.

Tell the kings and men gone by,
It's my time to make Money.

Tanya Raval

Mind's Mime

The day began with energetic sprite, a cleansing of sorts with
rose water and chickpea flour.
I bathe in milk to tender my body with loving lore; my
bosom is patted with a warm sun-caressed towel; I rinsed my
hair with the fragrance of the flowers,
The dress is special, a shiny silk, as if ready for a temple
treat.

The pots are put on fire, and the water-bubbling mist of
aroma saturates the kitchen with extracts of turmeric, ginger,
garlic, and tartaric.

A seasoning as medicine or glucagon, no longer a diabetic
moan.
No ailments come to me with apple cider honey tea.

A meal to serve the lord prepared, with spices, sweets, and
some Oeuvres greet the wanderer knocking my door,
An unknown face, a friendly tone, clean-shaven and dapper
clothing shown,
A new date this time, unrelenting to the negative push
But attending tenderly,
To my loving soul.

Who art thou, and where have you been?
My ears are ready to listen keenly.

I am prepared and ready to nourish this sight.

The butterfly alights so softly this time and zips away like the
swallow's fast dance in my minds' mime by chance.

Sight of Plight

Flowing flames of emotions in my sight
Nostrils flared, anger brimming up just a bit too tight,

Ears perked up listening to the devil's might.
Lips laden with unkind words to bite

A wrinkled face filled with passions so bright.
Holding back tears of uncomfortable plight,

Body taut, limbs already to fight,
Cacophony of demons in the mind,
Out of sight.

Treacherous is the sight,
Just walking on a straight road at night,

Unending mirages glistening all day in its might,
No bends, no turns, ups or downs too tight.

Forever, I must walk with my bipolar mind,
With thoughts and images already to rewind.

Desert plants flaunting their thorns,
Cut succulent plants, leaking juices mourns.

My plight, in the heat of the summer's sight
Tossing and turning ghost demons to fight.

Tanya Raval

Slumber

Come to me, sweet slumber,
Let sweet lullabies to my ear mumble.

A mothers embrace a father's blessings.
Let it stay in my lonely heart, missing.

Deep sighs to deep breathing transit
Let my limbs relax from this benefit.

A lover's caress, a baby in my arms
Open skies, under which I sleep in farms.

A life fulfilled and dreams of rainbow find.
Awaken at dawn with a peaceful and enthusiastic mind.

Why Me?

'Tis not the eyes that are weary,
'Tis not the head so dreamy
It is the body so laden.
In the darkness within.

Melancholic my mind
Wake up to despair.
Unable to repair.
The disjointed thought.

Keep me awake all night!
And make me sleepy all day,
Heart pounding so slowly
Every breath shallowly.

No meditative stance lost in the despair going south,
I may wonder sometimes,
Why me in these drudging times?

Tanya Raval

Stars

13

The cosmos of galaxies, the infinite space
What would it be to be in this gaze?

The expanding horizons of flight untaken
Lost in the myriad of things willing to be taken.

To become "I" in the vastness of many
So finite is my being, a thought so shady.

The ego has dwelled upon this reality.
Then why is my opinion seeking felicity?

Wanting to be and become the importance.
One among so many, fearing the distance.

The difference and the similarity of a point wanting to be a
star.
In the rhythm of billions bizarre.

Thoughts

Amid brilliance and accomplishments, the mind crouches to the
corner, remembering what was and what might have been if …

A story of the yester years' coming face to face with the
withering presence of the aged image, of lost opportunity and
time ticked by …

Was destiny overtaking the dreams built in rainbow colors?
Snatching the caterpillar like a preying mantis?

A chameleon changing shades to hide from the predator in a
camouflage unknown to itself?

Slouched shoulders and placid eyes,
Waiting to come out, unfrettingly, to bask in the glory of its own
presence of being.

My time too shall come, from the darkness of the cocoon, to see
the light of the day when everything seems just the way it should
be…

Fleeting moments of radiance and insight,
Willing me to change from within,
Into the might of the elephant's trumpet or roar of the lion.

I am the might and the king of the jungle, a Leo, and was meant
to be this way,
So I am in my full glory,
A fellow being in the cosmos of beings…

That is how it is meant to be. I for myself, me for others, and
we together, in everything universal,
yet identifiably unique and true to oneness.

Tanya Raval

Abuse and Love

15

Stalk her, prey her, frustrate her,
Until she gives up and follows you.

Then dictate, coerce, recommend, cajole, and play with her,
Until she succumbs and purrs, agrees, and is malleable to
Your needs, demands, do's and don'ts.

So, give her,
The list, the time, the money, the love, and let the luck
follow her.
PRAY THIS LASTS, FOR SHE IS DEMANDING,
unreasonable, boring, and predictable.

Unable to keep up and keep on doing the machine work,
Mechanically and masochistically,

To be creative, spontaneous, artistic, colorful, flamboyant,
So, recreate the ambience with luxuriant and ample love for
her.

Come Sway With Me

After seeing a musical mime with actors speaking about their hearts at the Stanford Dance Department, I tried to recreate the feelings portrayed using words.

Tanya Raval

It's My Heart!

Contorted body and arms,
Throbbing fingers held behind the back.
In a claustrophobic clutch,

It is my heart:
Stretching arms and legs up in the air,
Enlarging freedom- to give.

It is my heart,
Suffering in pain, with expressions of deep despair,
Outstretched arms, hands covering the face,
Hiding the hurt and abuse.
It's my heart-
Anguished sounds of pain and sobs
Heaving chest, up and down, collapse.

It is my heart,
So, before you give it away.
Like a butterfly flying away,
A bird spreading its wings,
A paw giving away some golden things,
OR
Break it....
Phish. Crash. Bang. Stomp. Grunts. Gasps. Shrikes and sobs.
Remember,
A light bulb in the head,
A spark of insight and understanding,
Conscious awareness,

It's my heart.
Throbbing, enlarging, flying away,
Escalating upward sway
On tiptoes,

It is my heart.
Lost in balance within the body,
Slow motion jerks and arrhythmia
Falling and shrunken to a fetus,
It's my heart.

What Is Happening There?

A crowd gathered in the street with howling men and women around a disserted lonely child, crouched in fear, huddled into the background.

"What is that?" They ask to a child in darkness of loneliness. "Why are you here?"

They do not see the parents nearby, so they are scared for him now! When they know not how he lived without them since then!!

The day they left him alone to wean away from them. Alone, into his play barn with a toy horse and a dog by his side.

"Why are they here now?" Leave him alone.

He spoke. "I have come to be me because of you and yours, unable to take me in your home or your arms but to beckon others to do this for me. Why now when I have learned to live by myself, alone, in the darkness!"

Tanya Raval

No One Should Be Left Alone

No one should be left alone in this life.
Gathering garbage just for a bite,
Do not leave me unwanted in a bin,
Scrambling for life you are unable to give,
The breath I fight for today,
May give you love and care someday,

No one should be left alone in this life.
With an empty stomach and a grated knife
The peace and quiet I am looking for,
Will be satiated with an open kitchen door,
A little food you spare today,
May become broad shoulders you can cry on someday,

No one should be left alone in the silence and darkness of life,
Your shared silence and courageous fight,
With their demonic devils,
May become their beacon of light,

No one should be left alone in this life,
With a broken heart and sleepless night
The listening ears and kind heart I find today.
May fulfill a poet's dreams someday,
A snuggled pause in a restless mind,
May reach its zenith and someday find,
Cures for your melancholy and depressed and bipolar mind,

No one should be left alone in this life.
With passions unabated and untold stories of strife,
The rise in their feelings they find today,
May conquer inequality and make Just laws someday,
We are all here together to fly our own kites,
But the colors in the sky we release or reach,
Should etch a landscape,
Without God in breach.

Visualization

The day has come to gather the dust around my feet.

Where did I wonder in the foothills of the mountains, among the clouds, beneath the white sky, in the hue of the heavens with grey condolences for the divine?

Where, your best creation destroys the beauty of your imagination's reality etched in the mounds of the rocks and the coldness of the warm un-melted snow?

The glistening glaciers, the melted waterfalls, rivulets leading to the sea leaving behind the clay on the riverbed with rounded stones and floating spores, moist pollen ready to burst into the energy of the blossom where the bee or butterfly alights along with the smoke from the burned down trees cut off from the vast forest greens of shades seen on the canvas before.

The light energy absorbed in the earth through the sky blue from the fresh rains, and the grey clouds get the silver bursts of breakthrough rays.

The rainbow imbibing the colors of nature from yonder to yonder, the circle of creation left hidden from my imagination in the underworld of ground beneath me.

Tanya Raval

Image

The blushing bride flushed and coy,
Hiding hues and colors of bright joy
Hidden in her pink veil,
A luminous burst all ready to unveil,
Meeting at the horizon gone yonder,
Seeking birth of creative friendship gone fonder,
Unmasked in her true beauty,
Held up high as a sky canopy,
The dawn has grown so brazen,
Nothing in this world is closer to heaven.

Beauty

The sky is a cobalt blue dress,
The sky has become a pink, grey face caressed,
Crescent moon a necklace,
The star a pendant in the nights embrace,
Hair fluttering in the wind
As leafy shades so kind,
Limbs of lightening all ready to reach
The thunder of earth in creative search,
For the beauty of God
In the Amarillo halo of mango juice drenched Sun,
At the horizon, a shimmering bun.

Tanya Raval

Creation

The new dawn, a yellow sky,
The fading full moon as silver fly,
The light spreading its wings,
Reaching the farthest frame to sing
Songs of fading glow
Of the bright blue sky,

The doves hovering over the tree,
Eagles gliding in the air as free.

Church bells tolling,
The fragrance of the wet, dusty winds,
Flaring the nostrils of deer basking,
Ears upright and anticipating,
Agile-footed and ready to leap.
Forward,
Not running away but frolicking
Towards the future,
Butterflies alight, and bees humming,
Nectar of creation as an overture.

Speaking Tree

Hacked, cut, beheaded me.
Shudders leaves, endure see,

Lost limbs and crippled me,
Stumps oozing nectar see,

Shocked, withered, now dried, see,
No water, manure awaken me,

Sleep or dead, so broken see,
No more green color in me.

I grow in circles, leaf by leaf,
Unfolding from the darkness reef,

My body bending every turn a dance,
Growing taller by the dark night's stance,

No worries of withering bothers me,
My succulents hoarding nectar see,

Stunted and plump,
As the hot sun dumps,
Scorching, bright, hot rays' sums,

Spawning my brood in the dessert's yellow night,
In the pink morning, I grow towards light.

In the vicissitudes of life, at the zenith of power and wealth, the evolved enlarged ego escapes from the realms of reality, of the limitedness in the vast cosmos. Far greater are the galaxies than our comprehension of our ego. The engulfment into the narcissism of one's selfishness enables one to be at a point where many things seem to be below our achievement, which sucks us down into the fall of a crater far greater than the nadir seen from atop. The rock bottom does not bear any semblance to the peak except our minuteness in the context of the Brahman.

To be aware of this always is what we need, to remain humble in our approach as to the next zenith we shall toil to reach. The gratitude of our supporters, well-wishers, family, and friends will always remind us to be thankful for those who were with us on the rock and rolling in the mud.

The oneness with the earth reminding us of our death in its ego form also merges with the elements. What becomes ether is the ego; what burns is the fire of our conscience; what becomes water is our heart, eager to mingle in the sea of humanity; what is the wind is the embrace of the divine power that enfolds us upon surrender to the ultimate purpose of our existence.

Eventuality

Now is the real time.
A period to find.
The newfound glory of the lord
Drawn out to bind.

Mind body and soul
In a flight
In his presence, at this time
Moment to moment
Becoming so bright
The future holds the eternal truth.
Of the absolute knowledge of Death

That shall be yours and mine.

Tanya Raval

Heavenly Finds

27

Whenever it is time
To dwell and wander,
Drink in the world as a nectar divine.

Like the bees and bugs
Butterfly or slugs
Slowly like tortoise
Or a sunbirds poise
Just hover and find.

The purpose of the shape
As my mind and body engage,
Feeding me even though I am blind,
To many of his flickers of magic
In the worlds of tragic
Or heavenly finds.

Sick Again

28

Nothing seems to be the same.
What is the essence of my being and name?
Who have I become?
A lack of confidence unknown to some,

Moody erratic and unclear
Everything swings away from near,
No one is mine, and I am alone.
To fight my own demons and moan

I have been sinking down this well.
And has my nadir come from hell?
How do I get up again?
Do I ask for help in disdain?

I must accept I am ill.
Then take this medicine Pill.

Tanya Raval

Believe

Jump up and above.
Don't stay in your misery or hove*
Physically and spiritually
Life is given to you to love.
Begin at it finally!

Like a
Woodpecker who gets at it,
Or a hummingbird who is better at it.

Drink in the will to survive.
Like a charging cheetah hunting alive

The oomph has to come back again.
I have to take charge and jump start before the tears rain.

Now is the time to seek from within,
No matter if the effort is thin,
The zest for life to live,
That is what I must believe.

*hove is an Old English nautical term with the meaning of moving

in a certain direction

Everything Goes Pouf

From the earthquake of counseling sorrows,
Erupted the volcano of untold stories.
Of love lava burrows
Bringing forth the crust of unveiled brethren.
Soot-covered faces of unmet desires from heaven,

Blowing from the bellowing mouth
The heat, the passion of the youth
The dark grey stuff
Covering the landscape of possibilities and futures goes
pouf.

Beating havoc of destruction of all efforts in its path
Before the calm comes from within for a bath,
The heat of sadness and anger must burst off forth.

Tanya Raval

Feelings

Hurt pain.
Sadness loneliness
A baggage with no gain

Despair, anguish, turmoil
Arise my anger, hate, abhor,
Dejected, burn and boil,

Blue purple patches,
Embossed as a collage on the heart repaired with thatches,
Rejected, abandoned, discarded,
Thumping red heart, spasmodic constricted,

Lost, missed, departed, separated.
Pushed apart, torn, and repelled,

Cut wrists and swallowed poison.
Depression, paranoia, psychosis, seclusion,
Nervous breakdown, isolation with chains, no permission,
Force, coerce, branding, taboo,
Sheep, sheep, follow, adhere,
Roads of asylums, identify you,

You, you, are that that.
Become, become!
The brat
Fight, tight, push back.
Kick, curse,
Abuse,
Give back,
Uh-oh,
Give up, succumb, concede, and greet
Tears, cry, howl, defeat,
Break the dam and let it out,
Let go, surrender, forgive and shout,
Peace, peace! sleep
Quiet rhythm,
Stay and keep.

The Desert Amuck

32

Sluggish summer's afternoon,
The hot air blowing through dawn and dusk,

Eyes drooping, anger flares,
No desire to eat, so all food to chuck,

Dry leaves fallen; grass dehydrated brazen.
All aflame as a whiff of charcoal husk

Amarillo skies glaze the sunset orange.
Dust in the sky spreading fragrance of musk.

Succulents thick, fleshy, thorns adorn.
No flower, just withering corolla that sunbirds duck.

Sleepy heads drooling past,
Waiting for cool thaw and rain to run amuck.

Lover's heat, smothering kisses and caresses,
All birds, bees, and animals ready to suck.

Tanya Raval

Passing Times

Hugs and kisses,
All the intimate misses
Muses of summer times,
Of pot grass and intoxicants fine,

Teenage years of rock and dance
Partying hard and daring a glance,
Girls and women, flirts, and their bliss,
Trying to hide their ages as Miss,

Wrinkles of times passing.
With sand dunes with the wind,
A landscape with windows and no blinds,
The clouds carry our mind's messages.
Looking in and looking out,
Emotions flowing freely out loud,

Untamed minds have achieved nothing.
Just Twitter or blog and random something
Hook up and jive: Facebook like a beehive
Nectar of youth sucking honey so fine,
Their future plans are all just worth a dime.

Realization

34

The dawn of realization,
Am I out of this civilization?

What am I barred from?
Why is it me who has to go down?

The world is round,
I am tied to the wheel so tightly bound,

Unable to accomplish any task!
Where are they coming from? Who asks?

What is going on with you?
Why do you sound so blue?

Tanya Raval

The Message

One time I am thinking of this,
Next time the thought of that,

It's a seesaw or pendulum.
Swinging with me to be a bum,

Articulating an intellectual symphony,
With the orchestra and the music of many,

Filling my heart to the brim,
Keeping my negative thoughts trim,

Passionate in my being so fine,
Melancholy is not mine this time,

Racing thoughts tick tock like heels,
At the footstep pace, making me feel,

As if the there is no time to dwell on loss or pain,
What do I get from remembering them again?

Lost in the myriad of thoughts,
A jig-saw puzzle in which I am caught,

There I go down the slippery slide again,
Which way was I supposed to take again?

Not wanting to leave this space.
What is it I am trying to brace?

An onslaught of emotions effervescing,
Do not stay in the head embracing,
Blow away the cork,
It is ok to be a dork.
Humble your ego and be vulnerable,
A message from my guru, the venerable!

Woe Be Gone

Doing this and thinking that,
This time, the cat is out of the hat,
Let it be known to all,
I am supposed to be mentally ill; after all,

Don't you understand?
When you try to reason with me
I am far too gone to agree with thee!

My manic state does not let me be,
My mind space is racing with Mr. Bolt, you see!

I agree to disagree every time,
Thinking of lying with the expression of mime,

Telling the journey from hilltop to the woebegone valley,
Dancing off my blue woes, with gyrations of the belly.

An important aspect of growth is to optionally suffer the pain, for there is no gain without this pain. Silence is important to understand the self and its subconscious patterns of thought. Meditation allows us to access the self during deep breathing and silence. The noise of the unspoken thought is vociferous in the beginning and subsides with the taming of the mind. Happiness is within our grasp, and the exercise is to help us stay in this space longer every time. But before we learn to access and tame our minds, the learning process starts when we disengage from the attractions or aversions in the unspoken thought world. Prayer and surrender to God make the journey a path of reliable trust and faith in The Lord.

Efforts Chime

The good days are over, and celebrations gone by
I sit alone with the stillness of my mind,

The thoughts of future now willing to fly,
Have come this far,
Willing my best to find and disappear.
Heartache, despair, pain, and loneliness,
Sinking me deep with tears of togetherness,
Radiating darkness out with light,
No more resistance to fight,
Fleeting sadness as in mime,
Motile moments devoured by time,
Success in my endeavor, as beating heart in wilderness
chime.
Within me, I shall find oneness with thoughts and feelings,
Seeking him, not outside but inside me and dwelling,
To stay comfort and caress my depressed, negative mind,
Brushing it away and purring rich affirmative words so
kind
Enfolded, snuggled, now comforted, I cry.
In happiness, for he shall be forever mine.

Tanya Raval

Embrace

Why would I want to escape?
The barricaded embrace of iron arms,
To chase the abandon freedom of the horizon's silvery
mirage,
A world in a marriage of hatred and rage
With arms entwined like the creepers grace,
All emotions seeking blessings like the thud of a mace.

Loving corners of these walls,
A resting place for the weary head as it falls,
Collapsing in the secrets of this bind,
After tireless journeys to find,

The fleeting peace as a butterfly softly alight my palms,
Drifting into the ears, as winds of psalms,
The strong, assured beat of his heart,
Matching the restless rhythm of the seeker,
In the locked looks flicker,
As the love-longed gazes start.

This Path

It was said and foretold,
That when they are with themselves,
Shit comes up within them from the fold,

The deeper they dive in this passage of journey to meditate,
More the layers of shit they peel off, while they regurgitate,

The thoughts of this mind,
Are so dark is what they find,

For him, the silence is peace,
A place away from the fast race,
A thoughtless world of nothingness,
When he is sitting silence, with himself in kindness,

And shit comes up for me when I interact with others in
noise without understanding.
And shit repeats itself, in rolling eyes by standing,
And shit continues to stay,
When I am the listener, as kind ears,
Notwithstanding the vicissitudes of bygone years,
Told again as bullshit,
In the light of lost ignorance and insight, at the surface
again as shit!
I need the sewer system to treat the untold shit,
A decontaminating "mind bug" to bite into the realms of
past unfelt shit,
Let the critter eat away this noise so that-
I am happy in silence with myself with others in poise
And shit, no more comes up as voice.

Tanya Raval

Mind Sounds

Silence, in the noise of the machine,
The unheard quenched signal of the background shine

In the mind escapes as the fleeting spark of innovation,
Willing to crystalize itself,
In a serendipitous discovery,
Of an idea to perform,

Immobilizing the pursuits of daily chores,
Until the freedom to dream,
Is fulfilled as a Patent on USPTO shores.

To benefit whom?

The egoistic capitalist for profit only!
Or the ununderstood nerd with his folly,

A lonely sociopath
Trying to walk the NGO path,

And the joy of becoming the image of your heart,
In the mirror of your realities fart,

Generates a cacophony of sounds,
As silence in your mind's mounds.

Happiness

42

Happiness is a burst of firecracker in your senses,
The euphoria of bathing in the Ganges,

A rhythm of patterns and colors,
A creative canopy protecting arms of mothers,
Happiness is.
Sounds of soothing waves and wind,
Curled up in ocean's conches and kin,
It is,
A feathered caress of tactile touch,
Tingling tongue with foods and such,

Happiness is.
Fire desire burning eyes,
Sights of sounds ringing the skies,
It is,
Gurgles of soda fumes in the nostrils as tickles,
The aroma of fragrant flowers giggles.

Tanya Raval

Love

43

Love came to me like the hummingbird as I hear,
In my nose, a tranquilizer dart,

A rose blossom in my mind,
My eyes all ready to find,

A church bell toll in my ear,
A symphony far from fear start,

Gliding my gait like a creeper,
Alight on me like a butterfly kiss, but deeper,

Climbing unto me like a tendril,
Embracing me like a dress with a frill,

Submerged with emotions, making me dance divine,
Drunken as such in love, just like wine.

Soul

Soul be not thou proud
Of your eternal being
For I exist and I die
Each day for you and me.

Soul be not so humble.
Lest I may be ready,
To cast you aside
In my ego to become "I"

Soul be not so lifeless.
That I may seek another
Body to be in,

Soul, be kind and generous.
For I, too, live in this world with Ye!

Soul is my food for thought,
For I may feel the life within Ye,

Soul be the liquor for my senses,
Such that I may let your cry escape through my lip.

Tanya Raval

With Gratitude For

Friends

Friends are for keeps,
They pull you out of the deeps,

They keep you smiling even in despair,
They are the hands whose help you share,

A touch, a peck, a greeting makes your day,
They keep you cool in the hot summer of May,

They share your time and season.
You do not have to share the same reason,

Supportive and kind,
Making merry with you until you find,

Your star, your rainbow,
Impulse that grows,
Like possessions of free mind.

Prayer Taught by Sisters of CJM

Just for today

Lord, for tomorrow and its needs,
I do not pray,
Keep me, my lord, from stain of sin,
Just for today,

Let me no wrong or idle words,
Unthinking say,
Set thou a seal upon my lips,
Just for today,

Help me to mortify my flesh,
And duly pray.

Tanya Raval

Final Journey to Heaven

Disengaged, Inactive, Conscious and Coherent
Preparing for his final journey apparent,

No need to eat or nourish, no need to drink,
As empty blood is at the brink.

Just sleep and beckon the horses,
Riding chariot of death forces,

Looking North
To the gateways of heaven,
Heaving six breaths
And the last seventh
On
6:30 AM of 29th and eleven……

Riding on death horses to heaven,
Meeting friends'
Gone bye before him, as per the raven.

Submerged in water and earth, his ashes.
On December 1st, his final flashes,

The thirteenth mourning on December eleven
Bye, Bye he now resides in his new destination heaven.

We love you DAD
Thank you for your life's teaching.
Pranam

About the Author

Tanya is the second-born child of a teacher and a scientist. Sandwiched in birth order between a bright older sister and a sick younger sister, much of her childhood was spent seeking attention. She is a sensitive and artistic person who was trained to be a scientist. Her many hobbies include all forms of expression, including dancing and painting. She has come a long way from darkness to light. Her feelings during the journey from sickness to coping are penned in these pages.

www.ingramcontent.com/pod-product-compliance
Lightning Source LLC
Chambersburg PA
CBHW060943130726
48001CB00003B/1032